Explore Space!

Astronauts at Work

by Deborah A. Shearer

Consultant:
James Gerard
Aerospace Education Specialist
NASA Aerospace Education Services Program

Bridgestone Books
an imprint of Capstone Press
Mankato, Minnesota

Bridgestone Books are published by Capstone Press
151 Good Counsel Drive, P.O. Box 669, Mankato, Minnesota 56002
http://www.capstone-press.com

Library of Congress Cataloging-in-Publication Data
Shearer, Deborah A.
    Astronauts at work / by Deborah A. Shearer.
    p. cm.—(Explore space!)
    Includes bibliographical references and index.
    Summary: Explains the different jobs NASA astronauts do on space shuttles.
    ISBN 0-7368-1142-7
    1. Astronautics—Juvenile literature. 2. Astronauts—Juvenile literature. [1. Astronauts.]
I. Title. II. Series.
TL793 .S4295 2002
629.45′0092—dc21   2001003437

Editorial Credits
Tom Adamson, editor; Karen Risch, product planning editor; Steve Christensen,
    cover designer; Linda Clavel, production designer and illustrator; Katy Kudela,
    photo researcher

Photo Credits
All photos courtesy of NASA.

1 2 3 4 5 6 07 06 05 04 03 02

Table of Contents

Astronauts 5

Early Space Travelers 7

Jobs in Space 9

Special Jobs 11

Commander 13

Pilot 15

Mission Specialist 17

Payload Specialist 19

Future Explorers 21

Hands On: Make a Mars Mission Patch 22

Words to Know 23

Read More 24

Internet Sites 24

Index 24

Alan B. Shepard

Astronauts

Astronauts are trained to fly and work in space. In 1959, NASA chose seven men to be the first American astronauts. But in 1961, Russian Yuri Gagarin became the first person to go into space. A few weeks later, Alan Shepard became the first American in space.

NASA

National Aeronautics and Space Administration; this agency is in charge of all U.S. space missions.

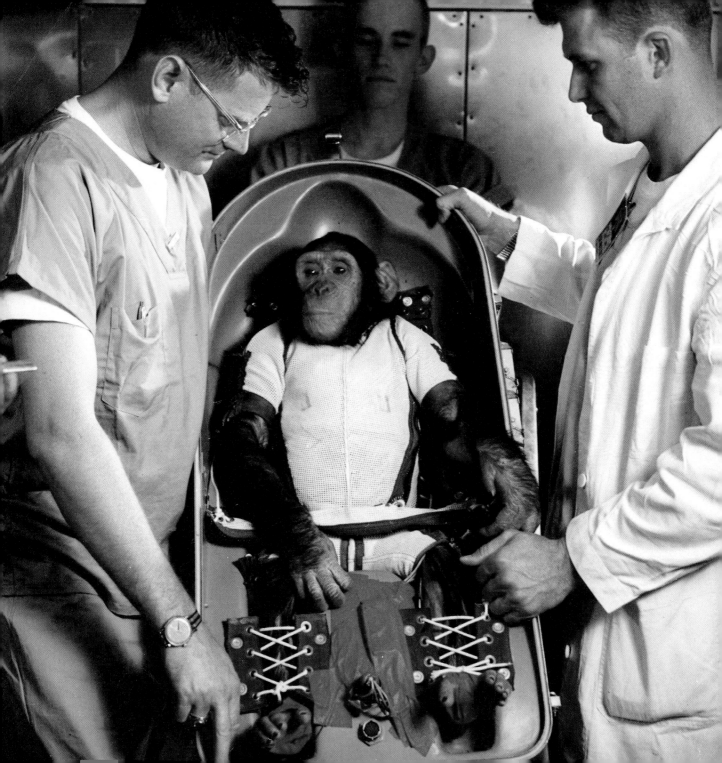

Early Space Travelers

The first space travelers were animals. Ham was the first chimpanzee to fly in space. Enos was the first chimpanzee to orbit Earth. Astronaut John Glenn later orbited Earth safely because of what scientists learned from these animals.

orbit
to travel around a planet, moon, or other object in space

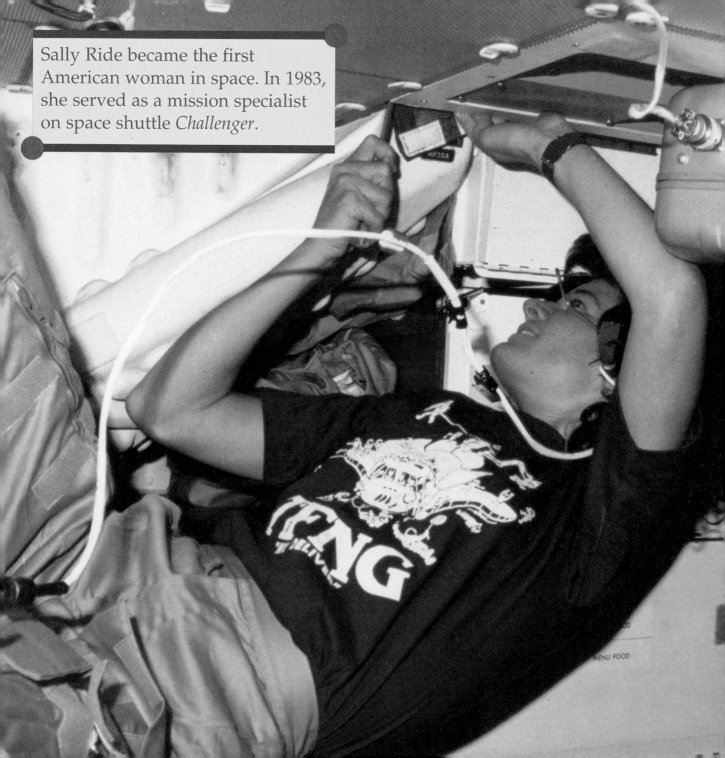

Sally Ride became the first American woman in space. In 1983, she served as a mission specialist on space shuttle *Challenger*.

Jobs in Space

Astronauts do many different jobs in space. They have to do the jobs of doctors when doing experiments on the human body. They do the jobs of veterinarians when doing experiments with animals. Astronauts need to be able to fix machines when they break down.

experiment
a scientific test to learn something new

9

In 1983, Guion Bluford became the first African American in space. He has been part of four shuttle missions.

Special Jobs

Four types of astronauts are part of a NASA space shuttle crew. They each have their own jobs to do. The crew includes the commander, the pilot, mission specialists, and payload specialists. They must work together to make a space mission a success.

space shuttle
a spacecraft that carries astronauts into space and back to Earth

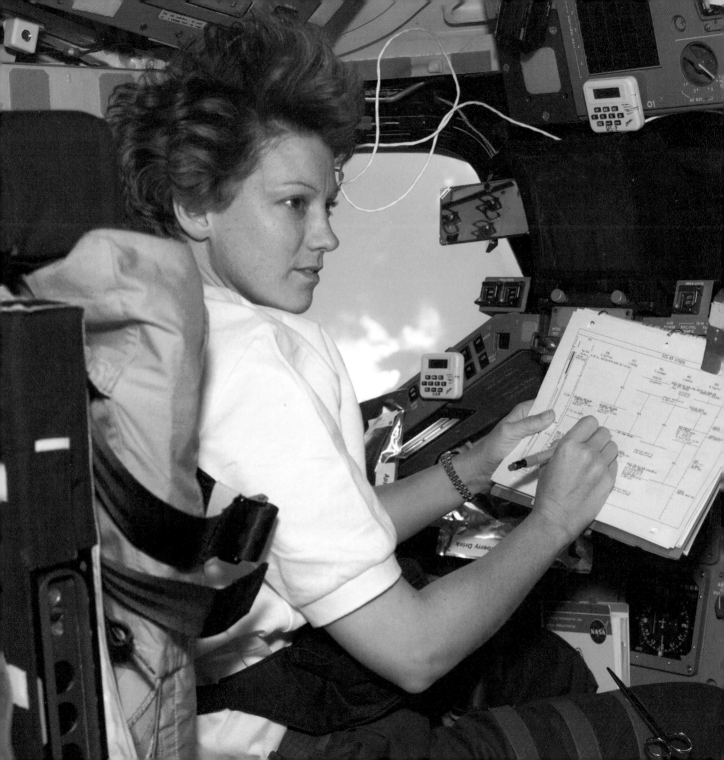

Commander

The commander is in charge of the shuttle and crew. The commander flies the shuttle and usually is the most experienced member of the team. The commander checks jobs done on the flight. He or she watches for the safety of the crew and the shuttle.

Pilot

The pilot helps the commander fly the shuttle. The pilot becomes the person in charge if the commander becomes sick or injured. The pilot also may use the robot arm to put satellites into orbit. The robot arm allows astronauts to grab a satellite and move it.

satellite
a spacecraft that orbits Earth

Mission Specialist

Mission specialists make sure that all the mission's experiments get done. They may study how plants grow in space. These astronauts do all the space walks. They may repair satellites or help build the space station.

space walk

a period of time spent outside a spacecraft by an astronaut to do a certain job

17

In 1962, John Glenn became the first American to orbit Earth. His next mission was in 1998. He became the oldest astronaut to go into space. He served as a payload specialist on this mission.

Payload Specialist

Payload specialists are not NASA astronauts. They come from businesses, colleges, or other countries. Their job is to do special experiments in space such as growing crystals. They usually fly on only one or two missions into space.

Mars

Future Explorers

Astronauts have a dangerous but exciting job. They fly in space on space shuttles. Some astronauts live on the space station. Astronauts have walked on the Moon. In the future, astronauts may go to Mars. When will the first person walk on Mars?

space station

a spacecraft that is large enough for astronauts to live on for long periods of time

21

Hands On: Make a Mars Mission Patch

Every astronaut team has a patch for its mission. What would your patch look like if you went on the first mission to Mars?

What You Need

1 sheet of white paper
Pencil

Crayons or markers
Scissors

What You Do

1. Choose a shape for your patch. It can be round, square, or any other shape. Draw your shape with a pencil.
2. Who will go with you on the Mars mission? Write the names of the team members on your patch.
3. What will your spacecraft look like? Draw a picture of it on the patch.
4. Draw a picture of Mars on the patch.
5. Color the patch with bright colors.
6. Cut the patch out and hang it up for others to see.

This space shuttle mission patch shows the names of the five astronauts who went on the mission. It also shows the space shuttle *Columbia* and the satellite the astronauts put into orbit. The American and French flags represent the countries the astronauts were from.

Words to Know

commander (kuh-MAND-er)—an astronaut who is in charge of a space mission

mission (MISH-uhn)—a special job or task in space; a mission may be a science experiment or putting a satellite into orbit.

orbit (OR-bit)—to travel around a planet, moon, or other object in space

payload (PAY-lohd)—something carried on a spacecraft that is needed for the mission

pilot (PYE-luht)—the astronaut who helps the commander fly a space shuttle

satellite (SAT-uh-lite)—a spacecraft that orbits Earth

specialist (SPESH-uh-list)—an expert at a certain job

Read More

Hayden, Kate. *Astronaut: Living in Space.* New York: DK, 2000.

Vogt, Gregory L. *Space Shuttles.* Explore Space! Mankato, Minn.: Bridgestone Books, 1999.

Walker, Niki. *The Life of an Astronaut.* Eye on the Universe. New York: Crabtree, 2001.

Internet Sites

Canadian Space Agency—KidSpace
http://www.space.gc.ca/kidspace/default.asp
Johnson Space Center—Astronauts
http://www.jsc.nasa.gov/pao/public/astronauts.html

Index

animals in space, 7, 9
   Enos, 7
   Ham, 7
Bluford, Guion, 10
commander, 11, 13, 15
experiments, 9, 17, 19
Gagarin, Yuri, 5
Glenn, John, 7, 18
Mars, 21
mission, 10, 11, 17, 18, 19
mission specialist, 8, 11, 17

NASA, 5, 11, 19
payload specialist, 11, 18, 19
pilot, 11, 15
Ride, Sally, 8
robot arm, 15
satellite, 15, 17
Shepard, Alan, 5
space shuttle, 8, 10, 11, 13, 15, 21
space station, 17, 21
space walks, 17